631art.com Presents:

"Losing Our Humanity"

A Book About the Crisis at the Southern Border

by Eddie Alfaro

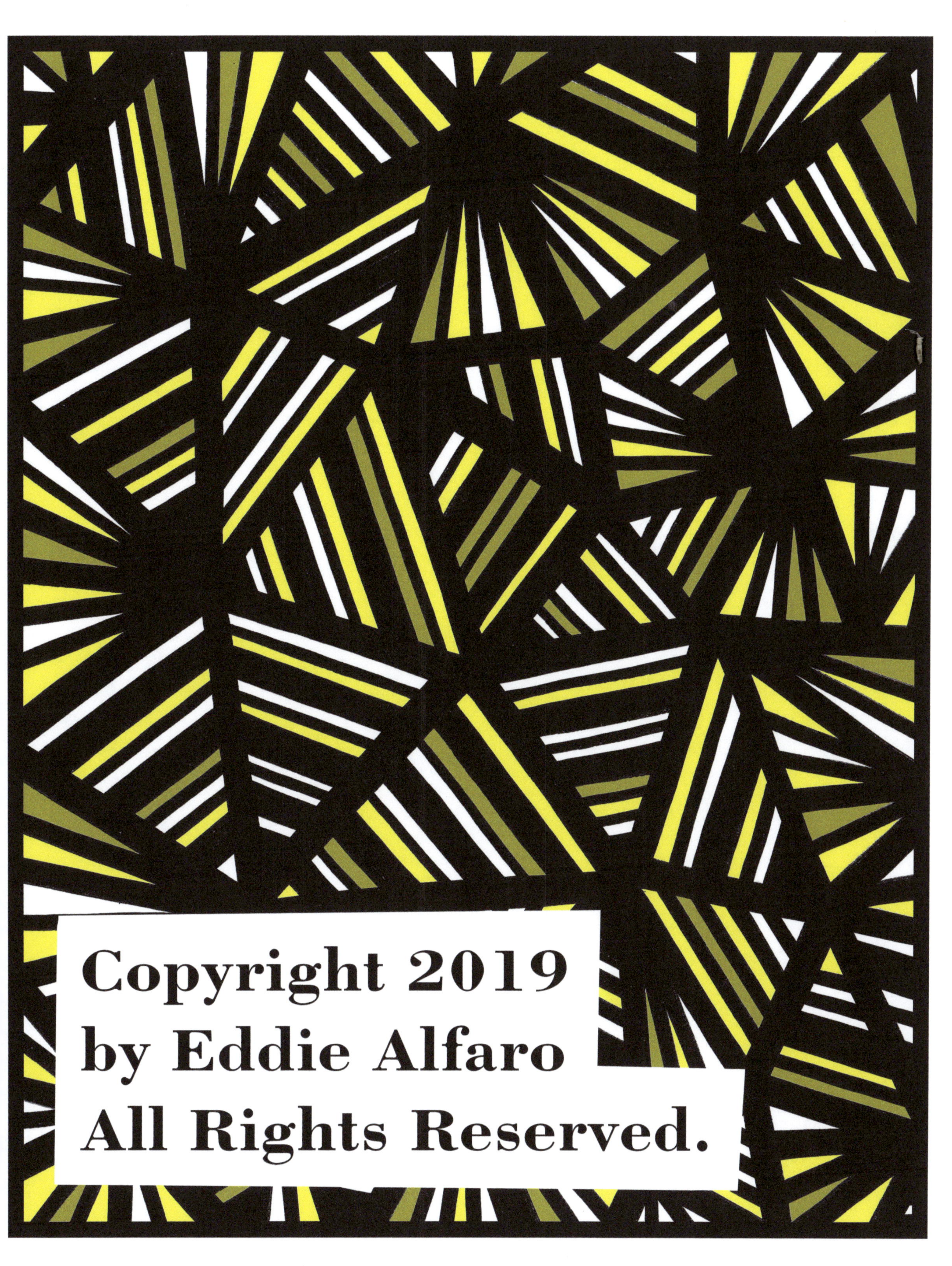

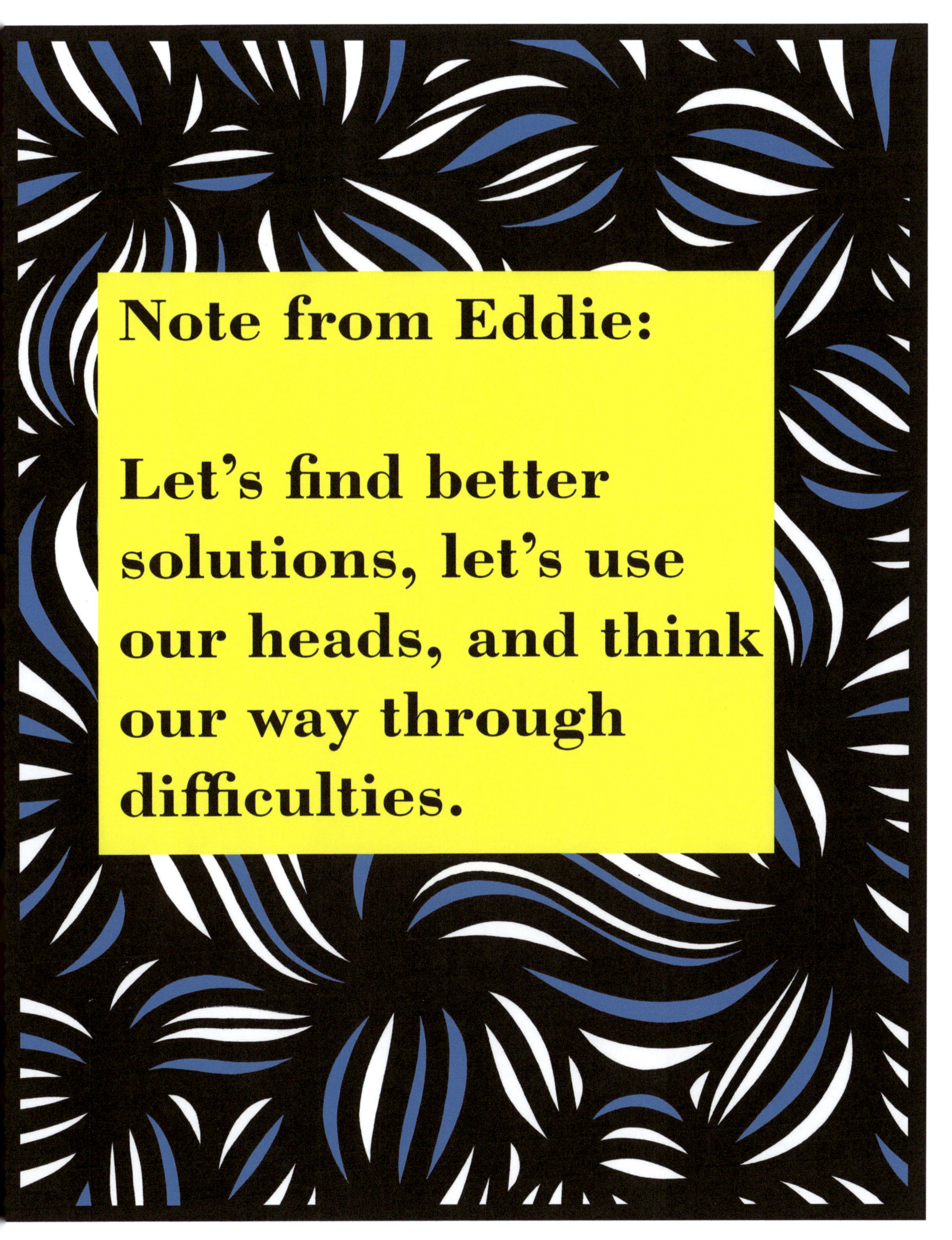
Note from Eddie:

Let's find better solutions, let's use our heads, and think our way through difficulties.

At the Border
Parents seeking
asylum are willing to
risk separation rather
than go back to danger
ZERO · TOLERANCE · POLICY

KEEP·FAMILIES
TOGETHER

FREE·the CHILDREN
NOBODY ·IS· ILLEGAL

NO JAILING KIDS
CAGING · IMMIGRANT CHILDREN · ALONGSIDE · THEIR PARENTS · ISN'T MUCH · OF · A · SOLUTION

STOP · THE · SEPARATION · OF · FAMILIES! ·
tHIS IS CHILD ABUSE AND A HUMAN · RIGHtS VIOLATION!!!!
PEOPLE · PROtEST · AGAINSt
SEPERATING · IMMIGRANt · FAMILY

THE TRAUMA OF SEPARATION LINGERS LONG AFTER CHILDREN ARE REUNITED WITH PARENTS

A MEMBER OF A MIGRANT FAMILY FLEEING VIOLENCE, HOLDS HER DOLL WHILE WAITING TO MEET AGENTS

HOME LAND SECU RITY.
The Honduran girl and her mother are taken into CUSTODY.

A GIRL CLUTCHES
HER MOTHER'S LEG WHILE WAITING
IN LINE AT THE BORDER

TRAUMATiZED
FAMiLY · BONDS
B R O K E N * . i .

FEAR, AGONY
A·MAN·IS·REUNITED·with
his·DAUGHTER·AFTER·SEPARATION

TRAUMATIC experiences...
SUCH AS FAMILY SEPARATIONS
OR INDEFINITE DETENTION MAY
LEAD TO MENTAL HEALTH
PROBLEMS LATER IN LIFE
HEARTBROKEN

INFANt · Ripped · from
Mother's · BReast · at · immigration
Detention · center, mother
Handcuffed · FOR · ResistinG.

REUNITE·FAMILIES
WOMEN·AND·CHILDREN
FLEEING·POVERTY·&VIOLENCE

IMMIGRANtS MAKE·AMERICA GREAt
NO·KIDS IN·PRISON CAMPS!
I CARE, DON'T·U?
FREE·THE CHILDREN
KEEP·THE·KiDS DEPORT·THE·RACiST

WE · NEED · TO · DO · BETTER
this · current crisis is · A · tragedy
PURE & SIMPLE

EFRAIN
DE LA ROSA
SPENT 21
DAYS IN
SOLITARY
CONFINEMENT
AT STEWART
DETENTION
CENTER. ON
HIS LAST DAY
HE BECAME
the LATEST
SUICIDE IN U.S. immigration
DETENTION.

U.S. SAYS
463
MiGRANtS
PARENtS
MAY
HAVE
BEEN
DePORTED
WitH
OUt
KiDS

THE · POWER · to · HEAL
tHE · POWER
to · CHANGE
Lives
THE · POWER
to · MAKE ·
DREAMS · COME
TRUE. + THE
POWER
TO
unite.
SUPPORT · REFUGEE &
MIGRANT · children

"WHEN WE REALIZED WE WEREN'T GOING BACK TO WHERE OUR CHILDREN WERE, WE ALL STARTED CRYING & PLEADING"
FAMILY SEPARATION TRAUMA UNDER TRUMP

Migrants
DESCRIBE
HUNGER
AND
SOLITARY
CONFINEMENT
AT
FOR PROFIT
DETENTION CENTER
MISTREATED

FAMILIES * NO
BELONG
toGetHer
DEMONSTRATORS **
PROtESt · TRUMP · ADMINIStRAtioi
IMMIGRATION * POLICIES

artwork by:

Eddie Alfaro

eddiealfaro.com

sponsored by:

631art.com

the
end.

www.ingramcontent.com/pod-product-compliance
Lightning Source LLC
Chambersburg PA
CBHW040140240726
48664CB00002B/548